HOCKEY
TRAINING AND FITNESS

DAVID AND PATRICIA ARMENTROUT

The Rourke Press, Inc.
Vero Beach, Florida 32964

Patricia and David Armentrout specialize in nonfiction writing and have had several book series published for primary schools. They reside in Cincinnati with their two children.

PROJECT EDITORS:
Dick Doughty is a former Elementary School teacher who now operates his own business. He coached hockey for 9 years from the minor level through Junior "A." Dick is a certified Level 3 OMHA referee and is currently Referee-in-Chief for his hometown minor hockey association.

Rob Purdy has been a Secondary School teacher for 16 years. He is a certified Advance I hockey coach and a NCCP coaching instructor. Rob has coached hockey for 10 years in the OMHA, with a Pee Wee championship in 1997.

PHOTO CREDITS:
all photos © Kim Karpeles except, © Nathan Bilow/Allsport: cover; © East Coast Studios: page 4

EDITORIAL SERVICES:
Penworthy Learning Systems

Library of Congress Cataloging-in-Publication Data

Armentrout, David, 1962-
    Hockey—training and fitness / David Armentrout, Patricia Armentrout.
        p. cm. — (Hockey)
    Includes index.
    Summary: Focuses on the importance of basic training in the fundamentals of hockey and provides drills and training exercises to help young players achieve their goal of playing better hockey.
        ISBN 1-57103-224-X
    1. Hockey—Training—Juvenile literature. [1. Hockey.] I. Armentrout, Patricia, 1960- . II. Title. III. Series: Armentrout, David, 1962- Hockey.
QV848.3.A75 1998
796.962—dc21   98–28403
                                                                      CIP
                                                                       AC

Printed in the USA

TABLE OF CONTENTS

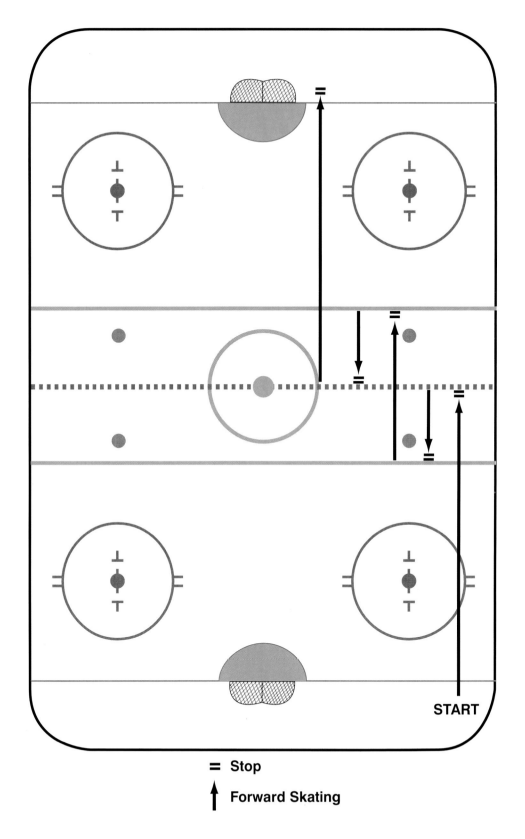

START

= Stop

↑ Forward Skating

This diagram shows line drills.

SKATING FUNDAMENTALS

Skates are the most important piece of hockey equipment you can buy. To be a good skater, you need the right pair of skates. Hockey skates are made with a combination of materials that resist moisture and support your feet. Before you buy skates, make sure they fit well. Walk around in them to test them. Don't buy skates that are too big; they will not support your feet, and you will not learn to skate properly as a result. Instead, choose skates that fit snugly.

Don't skimp on quality. Poor quality skates will only hinder your performance on the ice. When you have a pair of skates that are just right for you, you will be eager to start skating.

Skating may be the most difficult part of ice hockey, but you don't play the game without it. In the past, people learned to ice skate by teaching themselves. Today, with the increasing popularity of skating and hockey, skating classes are popping up everywhere. Hockey team training and practice sessions now teach **fundamental**, or basic, skating skills.

Fundamental skating skills include the **takeoff**, **stride**, and stop. You first need to adopt the right posture, or stance. For the proper skating posture, your skates should be shoulder width apart, your knees bent, and your waist slightly bent so that your shoulders lean forward. This stance allows for flexibility and balance. If you lean too far forward or stand up too straight, skating will be hard for you. The more time you spend skating, the better your balance will become.

★ **DID YOU KNOW?**

Most players want sharp skate blades that will grip the ice, but some goalies prefer duller blades so their skates slide easier in front of the net.

A good pair of skates are a hockey player's most important equipment.

Even the best players fall or get knocked down in a game.

Takeoffs and Strides

Your takeoff is important. It will determine how fast you get to a loose puck, an opening on the ice, or an opponent in control of the puck. At takeoff, your feet should be in normal skating position, the forward skate turned in the direction you are planning to go.

Begin with your weight on your forward skate, toe turned out slightly, and push off with the inside edge of the blade. Your leg muscles provide all the power. The next stroke quickly brings the back skate forward without lifting it too far from the surface. Lifting the rear skate higher than necessary wastes valuable energy and time. Before you've had time to think about it, push off with the opposite skate.

When you practice takeoffs be sure to practice the starting push with both legs. Give each leg equal time. Almost everyone has a weak side, so practice hard and long to eliminate your weak side. A hockey game involves turns in both directions so learn to takeoff with either your right or left skate in the forward position.

The first few strokes in your takeoff will be short, powerful bursts of energy; then you will change your movements to longer, more fluid strides.

9

Strides are longer, smoother strokes. With each stroke, you need to extend the back leg fully to gain great distance with each stride. You need to continue the proper skating posture in your strides. For balance, keep your skates shoulder width apart. Remember to bend forward slightly at the waist to help you move forward.

Professional hockey players practice skating for several hours a week. Skating long and hard is called power skating. Many youth hockey coaches teach power skating to young players. Power skating teaches skaters how to get the most out of every takeoff and stride.

A long, powerful stride produces speed.

Hockey players must be able to stop and change direction very quickly.

Stops

Two basic stopping methods are used when skating forward: the two-bladed stop and the one-bladed stop.

The two-bladed stop is used often, especially when skating at great speed. The two-bladed stop looks similar to a stop downhill skiers use. You simply turn your body and blades at right angles to the direction you're skating. You then dig the inside edge of your forward blade and the outside edge of your rear blade into the ice, and come to a stop. When you stop, your knees will be bent, or flexed; and you will appear like you are sitting in a chair.

You use the same principle in the one-bladed stop, but the one-bladed stop involves the use of your forward blade only. This stopping method leaves the rear skate free to start you skating in a new direction.

To make a one-bladed stop to the left, turn your body so it faces the left and put your weight on the inside edge of your right blade (the outside, or forward, skate). Use your left leg to begin your stride in a new direction.

SKATING DRILLS

Practice sessions help players learn the fundamental skills needed to play the game. Practice includes drills. A drill is a method of teaching fundamental skills. Drills will help you master basic skills and allow you to skate faster, turn easier, and stop more quickly. The better you can skate the more you will enjoy hockey.

Drills are a perfect way to start a practice session. Coaches have players warmup together using drills. Some drills have you start out slowly, then, later pick up speed. A warmup around the goal nets is often used. It is varied when a coach directs the skaters to change directions or to change the distance they are skating.

Coaches also use the figure-eight in many drills. Players line up, one behind the other, and skate from the defensive zone to the attacking zone and back again, forming an "8" by crossing at the center face-off spot. You skate the entire rink in this warmup drill.

Start behind the defensive goal. Skate to one face-off spot in the defensive zone, up the ice to the center face-off spot, and cross over to the attack zone face-off spot on the opposite side of the rink (so far you have made a diagonal line across the rink). Continue skating by going behind the attack zone goal, over the other face-off spot, back to the center spot, and complete the "8" at the second face-off spot back in the defensive zone. You continue up and down the ice without stopping after each complete "8." Your coach may call out a stretch or other exercise as you perform the drill.

After warming up you will begin other skating drills. Several drills are of benefit to beginning skaters who are still learning basic skating skills.

★ DID YOU KNOW?

"Pivoting" is a term used to describe when hockey players change from skating forward to skating backward, or vice versa.

Pond hockey is a popular winter activity.

Skating drills help you to become a better skater and player.

Backward Skating

Skating backward is another basic skill. It's true that some players, such as the defensemen, use this skill more often than other players; but every player needs to know how to skate backwards. Skating backwards seems difficult, but it becomes easy as you practice the maneuvers.

To skate backwards, begin by pushing off with the inside edge of your left blade and gliding back with the right blade (your left skate is forward). Then you reverse the steps, pushing off with the right inside edge and gliding back with the left skate. Posture is important when learning to skate backwards. You must keep your head up, your back straight, and your knees bent as if you were sitting in a chair. Don't lean on your stick for support.

While learning to skate backwards, you will need to learn to stop backwards! As you skate backwards, bend your knees a bit, point your toes to the outside, and press the inside edges of both blades into the ice until you stop. You can practice the backward stop with only one blade, which allows you to use the other skate to start a stride in a new direction.

★ DID YOU KNOW?

Ice hockey is two sports—skating and playing the game. Learn to skate well, with controlled speed and balance; then begin practicing game skills like stickhandling and passing.

Try this simple figure "S" drill to practice your backward skating. Start at the side of the rink at a blue line. Skate backwards the width of the rink along the blue line. Cross to the center line and skate the width back again. Cross to the other blue line and follow it again the width of the rink.

Crossovers

The **crossover** is another skill every hockey player needs to learn. You do a crossover when you lift your outside skate over your inside skate as you make a turn. The knee on your inside leg should be bent as you push off the ice with the outside skate. You will use the crossover to change direction and to increase your speed.

It takes plenty of practice to learn to skate backward.

This coach teaches a player how to do a crossover.

Many drills combine skills like backward skating and crossovers, or switching from backward to forward skating. Crossover drills might include skating around every face-off circle, or performing figure-eights the entire length of the rink. These drills help you perform both left and right crossovers.

You can practice your backward skating and backward crossovers with this simple figure-eight drill: Start at one face-off circle in the defensive zone and skate around the circle; cross to the second face-off circle and skate around it. This drill helps you learn to make tight turns.

Professional hockey coaches use skating drills too. Some simple drills, like the figure-eight, are used to warmup the team before a game. Other drills are more complex and combine skating skills, such as crossovers and backward skating. Professional players use these drills in their daily practices.

STICK DRILLS

Stickhandling is moving the puck up the ice with the blade of your hockey stick. It is a fundamental skill in ice hockey and should be part of your continuous training. Stickhandling begins with how you grip your hockey stick.

The proper grip: Your upper hand is the control hand, which is kept stable at the top of the stick's **shaft**. Your lower hand is your moveable hand, controlling your stickhandling, your passes, and your shots.

During practice sessions your coach will have you perform many drills to help you improve your stick skills.

Here are three simple stickhandling drills:
Drill 1. The purpose of this drill is to get used to the stick in your hands as you change skating directions. This drill should be performed first without the puck. The stick should remain on the ice throughout the drill.

The team splits and forms two single-file lines at one end of the rink. The first players skate toward the goal line at the other end. The other players follow. When the players reach the center red line, they switch to backward skating and continue toward the goal line.

Drill 2. The purpose of this drill is to practice stickhandling while keeping your head up.

Players form two large circles on the ice. Each player takes a turn stickhandling the puck around the other players in the circle. Players need to practice keeping their heads up and looking in the direction they are skating—not down at the puck.

Drill 3. The purpose of this drill is to practice turns while stickhandling the puck. A team will often split into two groups so each end of the rink can be used at the same time. Cones or other obstacles are needed for this practice drill.

★ DID YOU KNOW?

Goalies need to work on their skating and puck control skills too! They should be strong forward and backward skaters, so they can move in and out of the goal crease to play the puck.

Stickhandling drills help young players build confidence.

Hockey instruction includes stickhandling drills.

Players start at the goal line, close to the boards, and work their way close to the goal in the same half of the rink. Each player stickhandles toward the first blue line, turns around a cone, and comes back to the goal line. The stickhandling continues as the player skates toward the red line, around a cone, and back to the goal line. The last leg of the drill has the players stickhandling to the second blue line and back to the goal line.

Puck Control

Hockey is a game of speed and precision. Speed comes after mastering good skating skills. Precision is learned with puck-control drills. When players learn puck control, their skills benefit the whole team. For example, if a player passes the puck to a teammate who successfully receives it, the skills of both the passer and receiver benefit the success of the team.

★ COACH'S CORNER

Puck drills for the goalie—players aim shots to the upper right for catcher-glove saves, and to the lower left for blocker-glove saves.

Coaches often use simple drills for basic passing and receiving skills. Players pair up and skate the length of the rink while passing the puck back and forth several times. The drills are changed slightly as the coach calls out to the players to change directions or to skate backwards.

These types of puck-control drills are great for beginners, but the advanced players need variety and more challenging drills.

To make puck control drills more challenging, a coach will add game-situation drills. Game-situation drills force players to make quick decisions while under pressure; they must be able to "read and react." That is, they must be able to make the right moves without thinking about them.

Read-and-react can happen only if players have been in the same situation many times before. Actual games are not enough. But these drills can put them in a particular situation dozens—even hundreds of times.

A coach demonstrates stickhandling techniques.

Hockey players wear protective gear during practice as well as in the games.

Players benefit from these drills because they learn to think quickly and apply what they've learned to actual games. One game-situation drill has two offensive players skating along the boards toward the center line. A defensive player skates up the middle. A coach or leader passes the puck from the center face-off circle to either offensive player. The defensive player attacks the player who receives the puck.

Variations to this drill, like adding a third offensive player, can make the drill more challenging.

Players often get a chance to practice basic drills during a warmup session prior to a game. Take advantage of this time on the ice to advance your skating skills.

PHYSICAL CONDITIONING

Hockey is a physically demanding game. You need more than basic skating skills to play your best. You need to supplement your playing skills with total body conditioning. Conditioning your body with proper nutrition and exercise will increase your strength and **endurance**, and improve your flexibility and balance. Physical conditioning will improve your game overall.

Calisthenics and Aerobics

Calisthenics are exercises. You are probably familiar with many of the exercises and stretches that will help you stay in good physical condition. Conditioning exercises are done in most school physical education classes.

Some exercises that work the leg muscles include leg lifts and knee bends. Sit-ups and side stretches work the muscles of the abdomen. Pull-ups at a chin bar can help strengthen arm muscles, and pushups work the arm and chest muscles. Exercising your muscles and stretching before and after exercise are two ways to improve your physical health.

Aerobic exercise is another form of conditioning. Aerobic exercise gets your blood flowing, which in turn takes oxygen to your muscles. To benefit from aerobic exercise, you need to increase your heart rate for at least 10 minutes, but 20 minutes of continuous activity is even better.

Aerobic exercise will increase your endurance and lung capacity. There are a lot of fun activities that involve aerobic exercise. Swimming is one of the best aerobic activities.

DID YOU KNOW?

Are you looking for ice time in the summer? You can get together with friends and rent time at a local ice rink.

Outdoor rinks are most common in the northern states and in Canada.

Running is one way to get in shape for hockey.

Swimming a variety of strokes will work almost every muscle in your body—especially your heart—and certainly increase your lung capacity. Swimming can be easy to fit into a year-round schedule if you have access to an indoor pool.

Running is a great aerobic exercise that almost everyone can fit into his or her schedule. You can run close to home or at a school track. For a change of scenery, you can run at parks or on paved bike trails. When bad weather keeps you from going outdoors, you can use a treadmill indoors.

Nutrition

Hockey games, practice drills, and aerobic exercise will definitely give you a good workout; but there is more you can do to keep yourself strong, healthy, and ready to compete like a champion.

Help keep yourself fit with proper nutrition. You've heard it all before: Maintain a well-balanced diet by eating foods from all the food groups. Your body needs a variety of vitamins and minerals that can be absorbed into the bloodstream if you eat a variety of foods.

★ **DID YOU KNOW?**

What do the pros do to train off-season? They bicycle, use exercise equipment like a stair climber, visit a weight room, and stretch before and after each workout. But the most important thing any hockey player can do to stay in shape is to SKATE.

Normal physical activity burns calories. Added physical activity, like playing hockey, requires you to take in more calories. Don't eat "junk" food to increase calories; you'll only gain unwanted weight. Instead, eat more foods high in **protein** and **carbohydrates**. They will provide you with the energy needed to play hockey.

Two other important things you can do to stay fit are to drink plenty of water, before, during, and after exercise; and get plenty of sleep.

Nobody said exercise is easy.

In-line skating is a good way to stay in top form during the off-season.

Strength Training

Strength training refers to muscle building. For young athletes, strength training occurs with regular participation in sports, like hockey, and by including calisthenics and aerobic exercise on a regular basis. Weight training, or weightlifting, is not recommended for young athletes because their muscles and bones are still developing.

If you are below the age of fifteen, you should not use weights to build muscles; but there are other activities you can do. Continue calisthenics and aerobic exercises. These activities build muscles too. You can add variety to your aerobic workout by swimming some days and running on others. For a change of pace you can ride a bike. Bicycling is fun and it's a great way to enjoy the outdoors.

You can also take up another sport to improve your physical condition for playing hockey. Some popular sports include the **martial arts**, basketball, tennis and soccer. Or how about **in-line hockey**?

IN-LINE HOCKEY

In-line hockey, or roller hockey, began when two avid ice hockey players, Scott and Brennan Olson, replaced the blades of their ice hockey skates with a row of hard plastic wheels. The brothers wanted a way to practice their hockey skills off the ice. The in-line skates were a big success, and the Olson brothers then started a company called Rollerblade, Inc., which makes in-line skates and other skating equipment.

Off-season training is important if you want to be a serious hockey player. In-line skating and playing in-line hockey are two ways to continue your physical conditioning. They are also great sports to be involved in when ice hockey leagues are not in session.

In-line Equipment

In-line skates come in many styles. Some styles have boots made of soft flexible materials. Other styles have hard outside shells with soft inner boots. Some skates fasten with buckles and others lace up. In-line skates have brakes, unlike ice hockey skates. The brake is a hard piece of rubber behind the last wheel of one or both skates. In-line skaters brake by lifting the toe of the brake skate, which allows the rubber brake to scrape the skating surface.

Anyone who uses in-line skates needs to wear protective equipment. In-line skaters should wear a helmet, wrist guards, kneepads, and elbow pads. In-line hockey players wear helmets with a clear face shield or a face cage. Other pieces of in-line hockey equipment include a mouth guard, elbow pads, knee and shin protectors, and hockey gloves. The goalie will need a chest protector, legpads, and goalie gloves—a blocker and a catcher's glove.

★ DID YOU KNOW?

Roller Hockey International is a professional in-line hockey league. Pro in-line hockey allows body-checking. Many in-line hockey fans think body-checking lends excitement to the game.

Stickhandling is a basic skill in roller hockey.

Roller hockey is a serious sport that is growing in popularity.

In-line hockey is played with a hockey stick and a roller puck or ball. In-line hockey is a popular neighborhood game. Kids of all ages get together in vacant parking lots or at the end of streets to practice their hockey skills or to play games. In-line hockey is also a well-organized sport. The National In-line Hockey Association (NIHA) promotes in-line hockey across America. The NIHA has headquarters in Miami, Florida, and in Edmonton, Ontario. USA Hockey has also branched out to include an in-line hockey program called USA Inline.

The Game

To play in-line hockey, you need to know how to in-line skate. If you've mastered basic ice hockey skills, then learning to in-line skate will be easy for you. You use the basic ice hockey maneuvers when you play in-line hockey. You will skate backwards and forwards, carry the puck (or ball) down the rink with your stick, and pass and shoot to score.

★ **DID YOU KNOW?**

You can find books at your public library or favorite book store that are packed with stickhandling and puck-control drills. You can apply the drills to in-line hockey, too.

Organized in-line hockey games are played on concrete, asphalt, wood, or hard plastic surfaces. Rink size varies, like in ice hockey. Most roller hockey rinks are smaller than ice hockey rinks, with an ideal size being 180 feet (55 meters) long by 80 feet (24 1/2 meters) wide. The rink is marked with red and blue lines and has face-off circles and spots, just like an ice hockey rink.

There are five player positions in roller hockey: two forwards, two defensemen, and a goalie. Roller hockey is a more open game compared to ice hockey because only eight players skate the length of the rink. The players have more space for their stickhandling and skating skills.

There are in-line hockey leagues for players of all ages.

Roller hockey and ice hockey share many of the same rules.

In-line hockey skills include forehand passes, backhand passes, wrist shots, and slap shots, just like in ice hockey. The forwards use these skills most often. They are usually the best passers and scorers on the team. The defensemen and goalie work hard, too. Defensemen use their stickhandling and skating skills as they try to steal the puck from their opponent. A goalie uses ice hockey skills to stop and block but needs quick reflexes as the lightweight puck or ball can bounce back quickly in a rebound shot. Whatever position you play, you will need to have good physical conditioning. An in-line hockey player is constantly on the move and can't afford to get winded during play.

One skill in-line players don't use is body-checking—it is not allowed in amateur roller hockey. For this reason you will see more offensive skills in a roller hockey game.

GLOSSARY

aerobic exercises (air RO bik EK sur SYZ ez) — exercises that benefit the heart and blood vessels by improving the body's use of oxygen

calisthenics (kal es THEN iks) — body exercises that do not require the use of apparatus, or may include small, light hand weights

carbohydrates (KAHR bo hy drayts) — organic compounds, including starches and sugars, produced by plants and used by the body for energy storage

crossover (KRAWS O ver) — action of one leg moving over the other when taking a turn while skating

endurance (in DYUR ens) — the ability to withstand stress

fundamental (fun duh MEN tl) — basic or essential

in-line hockey (IN lyn HOK ee) — sport similar to ice hockey played with in-line roller skates on an asphalt, wood, or other hard surface

martial arts (MAHR shul ARTS) — forms of unarmed combat, such as karate and judo, that teach self-defense and serve as fitness exercises

GLOSSARY

proteins (PRO teenz) — organic compounds that make up living beings, giving energy, building and maintaining cells, and contracting muscles

shaft (shaft) — long midsection of hockey stick

stickhandling (STIK HAND ling) — guiding the puck with a stick

stride (STRYD) — long, smooth movement on ice skates or in-line skates; the distance covered with each movement

takeoff (TAYK AWF) — first move in skating from a complete stop, followed by strides

FURTHER READING

Find out more with these helpful books and information sites:

Davidson, John, with John Steinbreder. *Hockey For Dummies An Official Publication of the NHL.* Foster City, CA: IDG Books Worldwide, Inc., 1997.

Harris, Lisa. *Hockey How to Play the All-Star Way.* Austin, TX: Raintree Steck-Vaughn Publishers, 1994.

Smith, Michael A. *Hockey Drill Book.* Buffalo, NY: Firefly Books, 1996.

Stenlund, Vern. *Hockey Drills for Puck Control.* Champagne, IL: Human Kinetics, 1996.

Gutman, Bill. *Roller Hockey.* Mankato, MN: Capstone Press, 1995.

National Hockey League at www.nhl.com

USA Hockey, Inc. at www.usahockey.com

INDEX